Becky Carberg

# Watching the New Baby

# Watching the New Baby

## Joan Samson
### Photographs by Gary Gladstone

Atheneum 1977 New York

*To Brothers, Sisters,
and Next Door Neighbors*

# Contents

# Watching the New Baby

# Watching the New Baby

A new baby does some wonderful things. At first, they aren't things that are easy to see—like laughing, or sitting up, or creeping. But, if you are a careful watcher, you can see him do things he learned even before he was born. And you can watch him learning others so fast you will find it hard to believe. This book will help you to see and understand the many interesting things a new baby does.

You, as a child, are an important part of the baby's bright new world. A baby learns very quickly that you are special, different from grownups. This book will help you find ways to make him happy and to play with him right from the beginning.

I

# The Unborn Baby

One thing to keep in mind is that a baby is growing and learning for 9 months before he is even born. Inside his mother's *womb,* he lives inside something called the *amniotic sac* or *water sac.* It is like a bag filled with clean sweetened water. The unborn baby or *fetus* swims around and around in this watery home.

After 4 months inside his mother, the fetus is only about 8½ inches long. But already he has eyes, ears, nose, mouth, fingers, toes, and brain. He even has tiny eyelashes and eyebrows. In fact, he looks quite a bit like a little person with an extra-big head.

Soon he gets big enough so that his mother can

feel him bumping into the sides of his sac, as he swims around. She says, "I feel the baby kick." She is very pleased. Feeling him move is the surest proof she can get that she really has a living baby growing inside of her.

The fetus can't eat and breathe through his mouth the way we do because he lives in water. Instead, a tube called the *umbilical cord* runs from his stomach to something just outside his sac called the *placenta*. The placenta, which looks a little like the roots of a plant, gets food and *oxygen* from the mother's body and sends it through the umbilical cord to the baby. After he is born, the baby doesn't need the umbilical cord any more. The doctor cuts it off a few inches from the baby's body. What is left soon dries up and falls off, leaving a mark called the *umbilicus* or belly button.

Inside the water sac, the fetus doesn't care whether he is upside down or right side up. He doesn't feel the pull of *gravity* the way you do because the water all around him holds him up. He floats a little like a man in space, only he is much more graceful. For a few months, he swims and flips and turns, completely at home in his little world. He needs exercise, just as you do, to help his bones and muscles grow straight and strong.

After 7 months, however, he gets so big, his sac gets crowded. He can still get out of the way if, for instance, his mother rests a book on his head. But he finds it harder and harder to get comfortable.

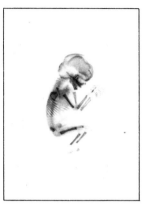

*3 months*

*4 months*

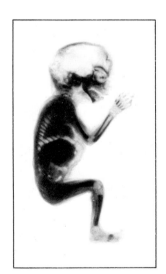

*5 months*

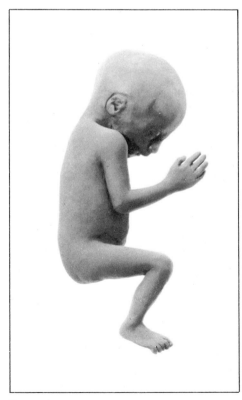

*6 months*

By this time, if you put your hands on his mother's belly, you can often feel the shape of his head. Your hands will make the baby feel even more cramped than usual. Soon you will feel the little lumps he makes with his hands and feet as he squirms trying to get away from you.

After he has been growing for 9 months, the baby is ready to be born. He is about 20 inches long and so big for his sac that he is forced to lie curled up in a ball, his knees pulled up to his chest, his head tucked down, and his arms folded in. His heart is beating so strongly you can often hear it if you put your ear against his mother. He is getting ready to breathe by breathing the water in and out of his lungs. He even has a little extra fat stored up because he will lose weight while he gets used to the outside world.

# Birth

One day, the baby begins to be born. The mother goes to the hospital. Everyone is eager to see the new baby. Will it be a boy or a girl? Will it look like its mother or its father or, maybe, like you?

Finally, the baby comes out of his mother. He is wet and slippery. He drags the umbilical cord behind him, but it is of no use now. It has stopped giving him food and oxygen, and the doctor will soon cut it off. Now, if the baby does not breathe through his mouth or nose as we do, he will not live. Everyone waits.

Suddenly, the baby starts to howl. The mother and father are thrilled to hear his cry. His lungs, which have never breathed anything but water, are breathing air. The baby is a part of our world now. He is not a fetus any more, but a brand new human being.

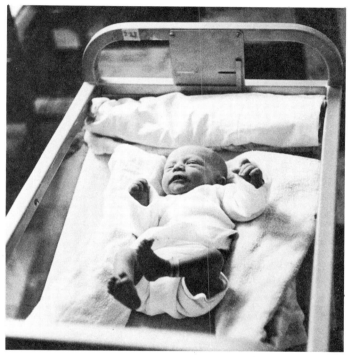

*Photograph by Michael Philip Manheim*

# Appearance

In his sac, the baby was covered with a kind of wax. This kept him from getting waterlogged—the way you do when you stay in a pool too long. The nurses wash off most of it. But little white flakes cling around its fingers and toes for a week or two.

The baby is born with skin a size too large. It sits loosely on him and sometimes looks wrinkled. He is all ready for the fast growing he will do for a while.

The new baby may be born with an inch or more of hair. Usually, however, this baby hair falls out after a few weeks. Then, sometimes, he is bald for months, while his family wonders what color his new hair will be.

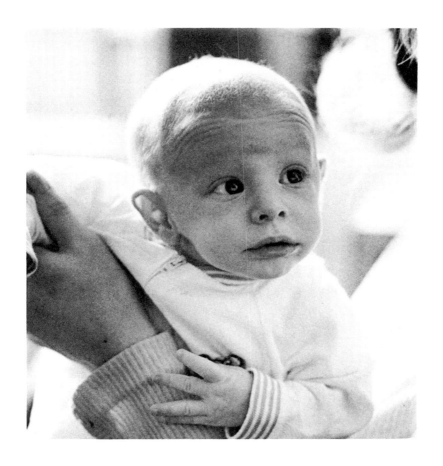

Often a baby's coloring is not quite complete when he is born. His skin may still darken some, and his eyes, if they are blue, may turn to brown. His eyes look huge because they are almost as big as they will be when he is an adult.

His head is also very large for such a little body. His brain, eyes, ears, and mouth all have to be able to work when he is born, and they take up a lot of room. On the other hand, his arms and legs are very short. His hands won't even meet over the top of his head.

The six pieces of a baby's skull are only loosely put together. This is because his head had to squeeze together as he came through the small opening from his mother's womb. Often, a new baby's head looks somewhat pointed or bruised from this squeezing, but only for a little while.

You can feel two soft spots on a baby's head. These are the biggest spaces between the pieces of skull. In a couple of months, the back soft spot will be filled in. And by the time the baby is a year and a half, his entire skull will be tightly locked together like yours, ready for bumps and falls.

The baby's bones are softer than yours. This keeps them from breaking during the time when he is most likely to fall. He can also bend easily in ways that would hurt you. In fact, although you must handle the baby very carefully, he is not as breakable as he seems.

His skin is so thin that you can see the blood through it. This is what gives him a reddish look. When he cries, you can see the pulse beating in his soft spot and in his forehead.

The new baby almost never has any teeth and won't for anywhere from 2 months to a year. His jaw is small until he begins to get teeth, and he doesn't have much of a chin. If he did have a big chin like yours, it would have kept him from curling up as tightly as he needed to inside his mother.

One thing the baby couldn't learn before he was born is how to get along with people. He doesn't know how to smile when he is pleased or to frown when he is unhappy. He looks out upon his new world with a blank face. Sometimes children think this means he is sad. It doesn't at all.

In fact, chances are that, if he isn't crying, he is quite happy. The new baby can't tell us how he feels, but he seems to be very curious. He seems to enjoy new sights and feelings. It's a good thing he does, since everything in the whole world is new to him.

# Touching

No wonder the new baby loves his first bath. Warm water is an old friend to him. He has lived for 9 months with the feeling of water flowing smoothly over him. In fact, his skin is not used to any other feeling. Everything else feels strange to him: the stitches in his shirt, his blanket, and the breeze as he is carried across a room.

The amniotic fluid was always warm and always the same, so the baby's body isn't used to heat and cold. When he is chilly, the baby can kick and cry to warm himself up. But when he is too warm, he has more trouble. His body did practice sweating into the amniotic fluid before he was born, but it takes about a month to get used to sweating in air. Besides, sweating does not cool the baby off unless somebody takes his clothes off. And when he cries, he only gets hotter. Since a baby can get very sick from being too hot, it is important to see that he doesn't wear too many clothes in warm weather.

The baby is born with a strong fear of falling. The womb held him firmly all the time. If you hold the new baby, remember to be firm as well as gentle. Sometimes a person tries so hard not to squeeze the baby too tightly that the baby is afraid he might be dropped. He cries loudly until he is handed to someone who holds him more firmly.

The baby won't know you, or his mother, or his father just by looking until he is about 6 months old.

But even in his first few weeks, he begins to sense differences in people from the sound of their voices, from the feel of their bodies, and from the way they handle him. If you watch, you can see that the baby begins early to act differently with different people. See if you can figure out what he senses that makes him act the way he does.

# Moving

The newborn baby feels heavy and awkward to himself. He is used to being able to move himself around in his small space. But air doesn't support him the way the water did, and his body feels heavy to him. He can't swim around. He can't even turn over or get out of the way if something bothers him.

Right from the beginning, he fights to learn how to move in air. He wiggles and twitches and squirms for all he is worth. It seems that he is getting nowhere, but, in fact, all the wiggling is making him strong so that one day he will be able to move the way he wants to.

For quite a while before he was born, the baby had to keep his arms and legs folded up. Right after he is born, it comforts him when he is tired to be tucked firmly inside a warm blanket because it reminds him of the way he felt in the womb. Some of the time, however, he enjoys the new feeling of waving his arms and legs around. And very soon, he gets to like freedom so much that he wants his arms and legs free all the time.

For the last 3 months inside his mother, the fetus was curled up so tightly that he couldn't move his neck or back very much. So, of course, when he is born, his neck and back are weak. When he is on his back, the baby cannot hold up his heavy head. And, if his head falls backwards, he can be hurt. This is why, for 2 or 3 months, you must be very careful to give his head special support when you hold him.

When he is placed on his stomach, however, the newborn baby can almost always lift up his head enough to breathe. If he couldn't, he would never be safe from smothering. He seems to have been born knowing that nothing is more important than breathing. If anything covers his face, he struggles and screams for help.

The baby tells us how he feels with his whole body. When he is happy, he curls his toes and wiggles all over like a happy puppy. When he hurts in any place at all, he cries and kicks and punches all at once. He hasn't sorted out the different parts of his body yet. He acts the same way whether it is his elbow that hurts, or his head, or his toes. In fact, he is just as likely to move closer to something that has hurt him as to move away. If you are a good watcher, you can see when he has learned to tell where each part of his body is.

Before he was born, the fetus would close a hand over whatever bumped into it—the umbilical cord, or a foot, or his other hand. If you brush the new baby's palm with your finger, he will grab it and hold on.

His grip is so strong that, with both hands, he can often lift his whole body. A baby monkey can cling so tightly to his mother's hair that her arms are free for climbing. Like monkeys, we are clinging animals. When the human baby clings to his mother's blouse, or beads, or hair, it reminds her that he does not want to be dropped.

The new baby cannot, of course, reach out and grab a rattle. He hasn't learned yet how to move one arm at a time, and his eyes haven't learned to tell him whether the rattle is near or far away. When he is 3 or 4 months old, he will start reaching for a rattle. Over and over, he swipes at it and misses. He is trying to find out just where it is in space. And, at the same time, he is trying to make his hand go to

just that spot. Finally, one day, when he's about 5 months old, he solves both problems and gets the rattle. And isn't he pleased with himself!

But he no sooner gets the rattle than he meets a whole new problem. Either he drops it right away, or he can't let go of it when he's tired. Learning to let go when he wants to is a whole new skill. You won't have any trouble knowing when he has learned it. He will drop every toy you give him. Then, of course, he will cry to have it back so he can drop it again. The baby does each new trick over and over and over until he is quite sure he will never forget it.

At 3 or 4 months, the baby learns to lift his head and shoulders up off the floor and wave his arms. At the same time, he lifts up his legs and hips so that he is rocking on his chest. He has learned to "swim" in air. You try it, if you don't think it's quite a stunt.

As soon as he learns to swim, he starts working on turning over. And he does work. He grunts and pushes with his toes. For a long time, he can't figure out how to get his arm out of the way. When he finally flips over, he is wide-eyed with surprise. Right away, he starts the new battle of getting back to where he started from.

From the time he is very young, the new baby loves to be held in an upright position. Like anyone else, he likes to see what's going on. But when some-

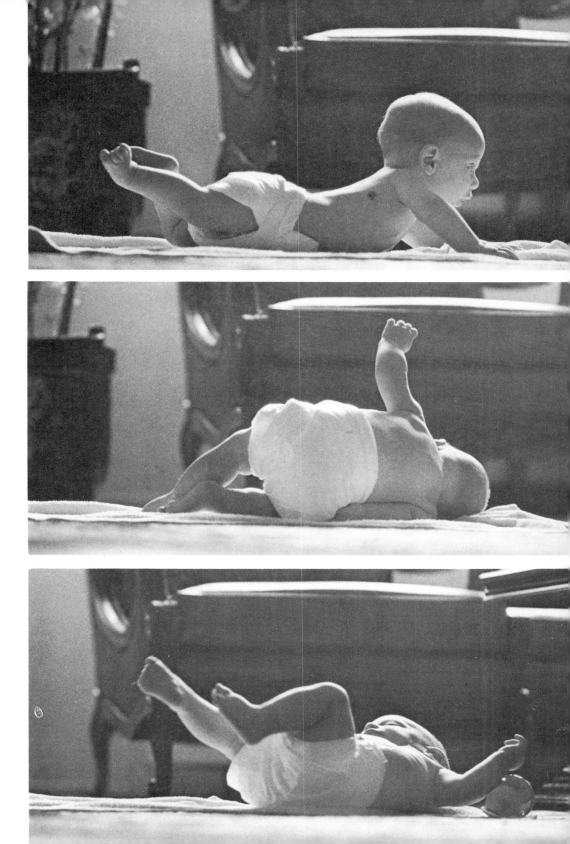

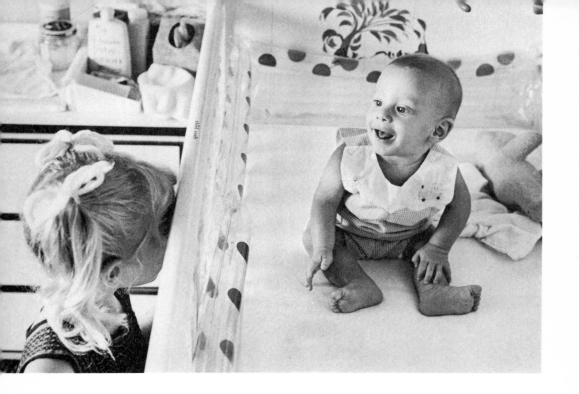

one first sits him up without something to lean against, he tumbles right over. He is eager to try again though. And again and again, until he learns the trick of balance and sits up by himself.

Learning to creep and crawl is hard work too. The baby squirms and thrashes until he begins to move along the floor on his stomach. Often, he finds himself going backward instead of forward. The more he struggles to reach the toy he sees in front of him, the farther away he gets.

The baby finds his round little stomach very heavy. He works for weeks trying to lift it up off the floor. At first when he does get up onto his hands and knees, he only rocks back and forth. He doesn't

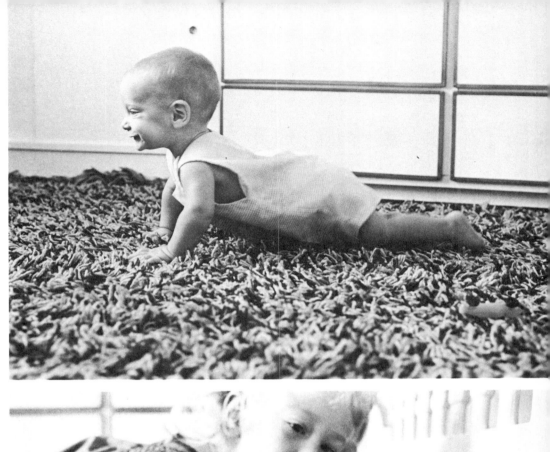

dare move a hand for fear of collapsing. But watch
out. It won't be long before he gets his skills together
and crawls. Soon he will be scooting all over the
house.

One day he pulls on the leg of a chair and finds
himself standing up. At first he doesn't know how
to sit down again. He either falls over or cries for
help. If you help him to sit down, he promptly
stands up again until he is quite tired out. But it isn't
long before he is walking around holding onto the

furniture. And finally, sometime after his first birth-day, he walks alone.

Most babies work on one problem at a time. One baby works on feeding himself first, another on crawling. One works on talking, another on walking.

# Seeing

A newborn baby doesn't look at you. His eyes slide around the room and stop in funny places. He hasn't learned to focus his eyes yet, so they often cross or go off sideways. For a long time this made people think that the new baby couldn't see.

In fact, however, he can see. But he doesn't have any idea what he is seeing. Inside his mother it was practically dark unless she was lying in the sun in a bathing suit. Even then there wasn't much to see, except the dim light itself.

When the baby is born, he must be quite astonished at all the brightness and color and pattern. The wallpaper is just as surprising to him as his

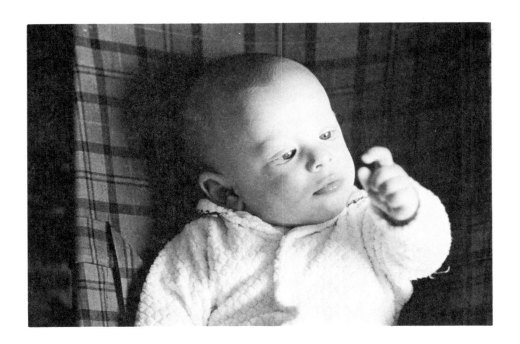

father's smile. He is as likely to study the pipes on
the ceiling as his mother's eyes.

Bright light hurts his eyes, but he hasn't learned
yet that closing his eyes will make the light go away.
So he goes right on looking at the light, screaming
with pain. You can do a new baby a favor by shading
his eyes from sunshine or bright lamplight.

A new baby doesn't blink as often as you do. Try,
just for fun, to see if you can go as long without
blinking as he does.

You can watch as the baby learns to use his eyes.
Watch for the day when he really looks into your
eyes. Eyes are one of the first things he learns to like.
Eyes are shiny, and they move. More important, he

31

has learned that nice things happen when eyes appear before him.

Very early, he likes to look at things that move. He tries to follow them with his eyes. If he is watching you, at first, he can only keep his eyes on you if you move slowly and not very far. It will be many weeks before he will be able to move his head to follow you when you walk across the room.

When people smile at the new baby, he stares back solemnly as though he were thinking important thoughts. But one day, when he is a month or two old, someone smiles at him, and he smiles back. Nobody knows for sure how he learns to do this.

Maybe he sees other people smile and learns to copy them. Maybe he learns that happy things are going on when other people smile.

The wonderful thing is that he does smile. He smiles when you smile and when his mother smiles. Often he even smiles at a simple drawing of a smiling face. This is because he is learning first things first. He knows the main outlines of a smile, but he hasn't yet gotten around to seeing the small things that tell you the difference between a real face and a picture of a face.

As if by magic, two strange objects keep swimming in and out of the world a new baby sees. They

are his hands. He tries to follow them with his eyes. When his hands bump into each other, he grabs one with the other, just the way he grabs your finger. But, at first, he doesn't even know that what he is grabbing is the same object he is seeing.

It takes him quite a while to learn to play with his hands whenever he wants to. When he can do this, he has learned three things, none of them easy. He has learned to move his hands to a place where he can see them, to hold them there, and to keep his eyes on them.

# Hearing

There may not be much to see in the womb, but there is plenty to hear. A fetus hears most of the things you hear, in a muffled sort of way. He also hears some funny things. When his mother coughs or burps or drinks ginger ale, it sounds like thunder to him. During much of the day, the murmur of his mother's voice keeps him company. And all the time, day or night, he hears his mother's heart beating like a loud drum.

After he is born, the baby is alarmed by silence. He can be comforted by a ticking clock, the whirr of a washing machine, or the rumble of a car motor. He likes any sound that reminds him of the steady sounds of his mother's body. He likes to be talked to softly, although, of course, he doesn't understand words. And he likes to be picked up and held close where he can hear the heartbeat he is used to.

The baby is born with rhythm. He is used to the rhythm of his mother's heart, the rhythm of her breathing, the rhythm of her walking. If you watch the baby, you will see that he often waves his hands and feet to a rhythm all his own. He cries with rhythm too. No wonder he almost always likes music.

# Eating

Inside his mother, the fetus gets almost all of its food through the umbilical cord. So how do his mouth and stomach know how to work right from the minute he is born?

The answer is that every day the fetus drinks a lot of the amniotic fluid. He gets very good at swallowing. The fluid is digested by his body almost the way milk will be digested after he is born. He gets a little food from the fluid. But mostly his body practices on it.

Often a fetus is so greedy as he gulps down the fluid that he gets the hiccups. The mother feels her baby jerking every few seconds inside of her. Most newborn babies hiccup quite a lot too.

If a new baby did not know how to suck as well as to swallow, he could not get milk from the breast or bottle. Until doctors learned to feed babies through a tube, a baby who sucked poorly often died because he could not get enough to eat. So the fetus also practices sucking. He bumps into the umbilical cord as he swims around and stops to suck on that for a while. Sometimes he finds his thumb or a toe and sucks on it.

Just to be on the safe side, babies are often born wanting to suck more than enough to get the milk they need. Often, a baby wants to suck practically all the time he is awake. But, since he can't usually control his arms well enough to put his thumb into his mouth whenever he wants to, he has a hard time. He can only cry for help. You can often comfort a fretful baby by giving him something to suck on and returning it every time he loses it.

A baby's mouth is the most highly trained part of his body. Not only can the baby suck and swallow, he can also find anything that touches his cheek or chin or lips. He nuzzles around until he gets all sorts of things into his mouth—a corner of his blanket, his own hands, your finger, even his toes sometimes. If his mouth did not know how to find and hold onto the nipple, he would have trouble getting his milk.

The baby's mouth tells him more about a strange object than his eyes or his ears or his hands do. As soon as he can, he will put everything he gets hold

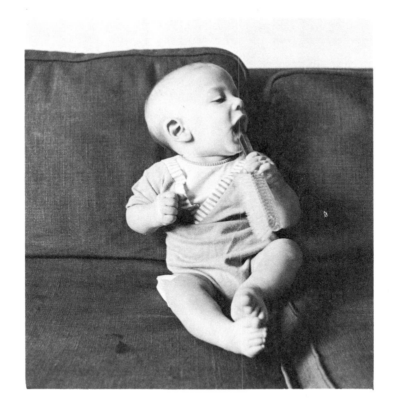

of into his mouth. Whatever it is just might turn out to be food. But, just as important, he uses his mouth the way you use your eyes—to tell him about his world.

Within an hour of being born, the baby will usually stop crying and settle down to suck at his mother's breast or a bottle as if he had been doing it forever. He knows how to find the nipple, suck, swallow, and digest. This is the moment he has been practicing for.

Actually, for a couple of days, the new baby is too tired from being born to do much but sleep. On about the third day, however, he wakes up very hungry. By this time, lots of milk is coming into his mother's breasts—sometimes so much that it spurts into the baby's mouth without his doing very much work at all.

The umbilical cord fed the fetus so well that he felt very little hunger. And he could swallow amniotic fluid whenever he felt like it. The new baby is not happy at all to find that he can only eat when his mother is ready to feed him. The hunger he feels is not only painful to him, it is also very frightening. He has no way of knowing that some-one will feed him when he needs food.

At first, the baby screams with hunger every couple of hours, day and night. Luckily, even before he was born, he was used to being waked up more often in the daytime than at night when his mother slept. He also learns the ways of our world quickly. So, before long, he sleeps a lot more at night than during the day.

Some babies are hungrier than others. But most want feedings at about the same times each day, any-where from 2 to 5 hours apart. Since the baby changes from week to week, his mother usually tries to feed him when he seems hungry.

If the baby drinks more than he needs, he just spits it up again. This is very simple for him. It is not like vomiting and does not mean that he is sick in any way. He also gulps a lot of air when he is drinking or crying. An air bubble in his stomach makes a baby uncomfortable. You can burp him or help him get the air up by patting his back.

A mother who feeds her baby from her breasts is said to *nurse* her baby. Once she gets started, it is pleasant and easy for her. She has warm, clean milk ready for the baby anytime, anywhere. Nursing also helps her get slim again after having the baby.

A mother's milk is thinner and sweeter than cow's milk. It is the safest and best food for the new baby. He almost never gets sick on his mother's milk, although he sometimes does on other milk. As time goes by, the mother's milk changes to meet the changing needs of the baby.

The mother's breasts make as much or as little milk as the baby needs. If he empties the breasts one day, they make more milk for him the next day. If he leaves a lot one day, they make less milk the next day. A woman can usually even nurse twins if she wants to. When she stops nursing her baby, she does so a little at a time until her breasts stop making milk. When the baby drinks all of his milk from a bottle or cup, he is said to be *weaned* from the breast.

As you can see, a mother cannot leave her baby for very long at a time if she nurses him. Although cow's milk is not as good for the baby as mother's milk, it makes him feel full for longer. Because of this, the bottle-fed baby does not have to be fed as

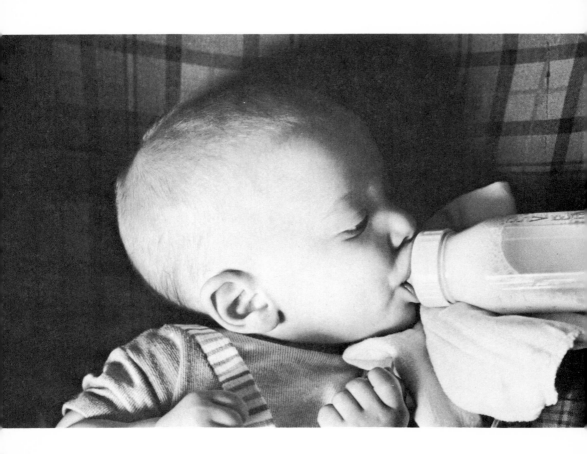

often as the breast-fed baby. In the United States, many mothers feel it is easier not to nurse their babies. Others are afraid they will not have enough milk. These mothers feed their babies from bottles filled with cow's milk or with special *formula*.

Milk or formula is the baby's most important food for at least a year. But when he is between a month and four months old, he begins to eat a little solid food as well.

When his mother shoves in the very first spoonful of cereal or strained fruit, the baby doesn't know what is going on. He has every reason to think that milk is the only food in the world. He shoves the cereal around his mouth with his tongue, feeling it. Then he spits it out and lets it dribble down his chin. Soon he swallows a little and makes a face. But he learns fast. After a few days, he finds that cereal makes him feel good just the way milk does. Soon he swallows almost as much as he drips onto his bib.

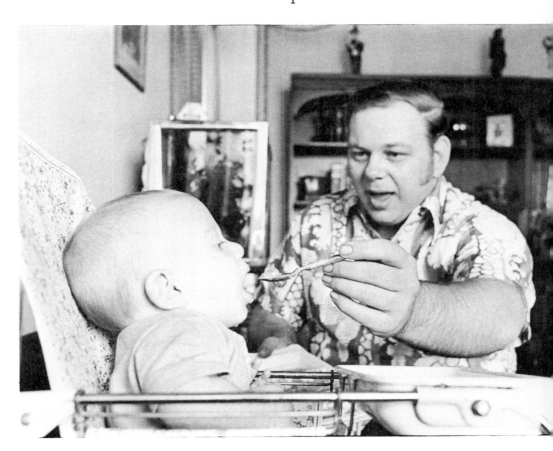

At first the baby cares more what his food feels like than what it tastes like. Then one day he gets fussy. He likes carrots but can't stand spinach. He likes apple sauce but spits out liver. This is because his sense of smell is getting sharper and helping him to taste things.

Most small babies wet their diapers about every half hour. They do not have enough control yet to stay dry even if they wanted to. Some babies move their bowels only once every few days. Others do so six or seven times a day. All babies need to have their diapers changed often, though, because their skin is so tender they easily get rashes.

# Sleeping

When his mother walks, the fetus sleeps comfortably in his swinging sac. But when, in the last months of pregnancy, she lies down on her back to rest, he finds himself lying right on her jagged backbone. He squirms and twists, trying to get comfortable. His mother isn't happy either. When she gets up, she says, "The baby kept me awake all night with his kicking."

After he is born, the baby is upset to find that his new bed doesn't move. It doesn't walk, or talk, or even breathe. The silence and stillness seem as spooky to the baby as it would seem to you to find yourself in a dark cramped place listening to the

45

deep boom of a heartbeat. You can often make the new baby feel more at home by rocking or jiggling his bed. Almost every baby loves to be bounced along a street in his carriage. Noise and movement don't bother him. That's what he's used to, and that's what he likes.

Some babies sleep most happily on their backs; others, on their sides or stomachs. If you watch a baby carefully, you will soon learn how he feels most comfortable. When he does not have clothes or blankets getting in his way, the new baby will sometimes curl up in the same way he did inside his mother. The fetus sleeps 16 to 20 hours a day, but not all at once. He wakes up many times to take a swallow or two of fluid or to turn over. His mother often wakes him up by running to catch a bus or banging pots while she is making supper.

Your habit of sleeping all night long without a single thing to eat seems cruel to the new baby. He gets hungry and bored. He cries until his mother wakes up and feeds him. Then, sometimes, he wants to play.

His mother, who is tired from his birth, has a hard time getting enough sleep. This is why the mother of a new baby sometimes can't help being a bit cranky. It is also why people often ask her, "Is the baby sleeping through the night yet?" When he is anywhere from 1 to 6 months old, the answer will finally be "yes," and the mother's temper will get better.

Some babies sleep most of the time. Others like to be awake quite a bit—watching and hearing and feeling their new world. For a few weeks, the new baby spends part of his time not quite awake and not quite asleep. He looks as though he is dreaming about the world he has left behind.

A tired baby will usually fall asleep wherever he is. Sometimes, though, when there is company or a lot going on, a baby gets overexcited and can't go to sleep or even drink his milk. He cries and cries. Sometimes if he is walked up and down in a quiet room, he will calm down enough to nurse and go to sleep.

# Crying

New babies make many sounds. They cough, sneeze, burp, yawn, hiccup, and cry. But most of all, they cry, or at least it seems that way.

Doctors have learned an amazing thing. The fetus cries in the womb. We can't usually hear him because only water passes his *vocal cords*. A few times, however, doctors have injected air into a baby's sac and heard an unborn baby crying within his mother.

When you stop to think about it, crying is one of the most important skills the fetus practices. For a long time after he is born, the baby cries to clear out anything in his windpipe that might choke him.

Just as important, crying is the only way the baby

has of saying, "Here I am. Please look after me." If he could not cry, a mother would have no way of knowing when she should rush to help him and when she should leave him alone.

At first, the baby always cries in the same way, "Waa, waa, waa." He has no control over the sound he makes. Whether he is hungry or cold or hot or hurt or bored, his cries sound alike. Luckily, since a new baby cries so much, his eyes don't make tears for at least 5 or 6 weeks.

Since a baby needs a lot of help to live, he needs a way to command people to look after him. He has it. The cry of a new baby is one of the most difficult sounds on earth for a human being to listen to. Most grownups just can't sit still while a baby cries. They are cross and jumpy until he stops.

This makes it very difficult for parents when they can't figure out why the baby is crying. And, during the first 3 months, the baby sometimes cries when nothing seems to be wrong. He cries when he doesn't need food or sucking or a blanket or sleep or a cuddle. He just cries. Nothing pleases him.

When he does a lot of this strange crying, he is said to have *colic*. People don't agree as to what causes colic. But they do agree that listening to a colicky baby almost drives them crazy. They have an awful time knowing when he really needs something and when he is just crying.

No new baby has an easy life. When he cries, nobody understands what he is trying to say. When he is hungry, someone tries to play with him. When he is tired, someone tries to feed him. When he wants to play, someone tries to put him to bed.

No wonder he soon learns to cry in different ways when he is hungry and when he is tired. If you listen carefully in the baby's second and third months, you will begin to understand what he wants.

One day, the baby makes a noise that isn't crying. He is surprised at himself and tries to do it again. He begins to gurgle and coo and chirp. When you talk

to him, he talks back.

If you are a good listener, as the months go by you can hear him finding the sounds he will need to talk. First he makes the vowel sounds. Then he gurgles way back in his throat, making *g* and *k* and *y* sounds. Then he finds his tongue and begins to sing *la* and *ta* and *da da,* much to his father's delight. Finally, he starts to use his lips, making *b* and *p* and *m* sounds. Most babies say "da-da" before they say "mama."

One of the nicest things you can do for a baby of any age is to talk to him. He likes to hear his own sounds repeated back to him. He likes to have you tell him what he is doing and what you are doing long before he can understand a word. Talking to the baby makes him interested in talking. He is learning from you that he will soon talk too. Don't be in a hurry, though. Most babies don't say much before they are about 18 months old.

# Loving

The brand new baby does not know about love. But, as you have seen, he does like the warmth and rhythm and movement of being held. He is also curious. He wants to be where he can watch people all the time. He may not know about love, but he knows when he is lonely, and he knows when he is bored.

He is all ready to learn about love. But he can't learn alone. People have to show him. Every time you touch or cuddle or talk to the new baby, you are teaching him about love. And he will never learn anything more important.

In fact, you can teach the baby about love and

about his new world even better than most grown-ups can. For, before he is old enough to play with a toy or to understand a word, he begins to like being around other children. Maybe this is because they move around so quickly, or because their faces are close to his, or because their voices are different from those of grownups. Maybe it is because children don't have to be told that a new baby is a real person with a name and a being all his own.

Whatever the reason is, you, as a child, are a special person to the baby many months before he is big enough to play with you. When he rests his solemn eyes on you, even before he learns to smile, maybe he already knows he wants to be your friend.

# When Will
# the Baby Smile?

Here is a list that tells when most babies *start* to do certain things. Of course, every baby is different. Very few babies will do everything at exactly the age suggested by the list. A baby usually works on one group of things at a time. A baby who crawls and sits up late will often say words early, and the other way around.

It is fun to watch a baby grow up. But remember that the age at which he first walks or crawls has very little to do with how well he will get along in life. The really important questions are these: Is he happy? Does he like people? Does he know that he is loved?

GRASPS

From birth, the baby grasps anything that brushes his palm. He stops doing this at about 4 months, when he begins to pick things up on purpose.

LIFTS HEAD

Birth–2 months—When placed on his stomach, he lifts his head and looks around.

SMILES

2–3 months—Even before he can smile back, he starts to show that he is pleased when someone smiles at him. (From birth, a baby makes a funny smiling face by accident sometimes, especially when he needs to burp.)

CRIES TEARS

2–3 months.

PUTS HANDS IN MOUTH WHENEVER HE WANTS TO

2–3 months—Even now, he can't usually find his thumb but settles for whichever piece of hand gets to his mouth first. (From birth, a baby sucks on his hand if he happens to find it near his mouth.)

HOLDS UP HEAD

2–4 months—Support the baby's head until you are absolutely SURE he can support it himself.

LAUGHS

3–4 months—The baby begins to laugh when you tickle him gently or make faces at him.

## GURGLES

3-4 months—He begins to make a lot of noises just for fun. He loves to be talked to and begins to "talk" back.

## KNOWS MOTHER

About 4 months. (Can you see how he shows that he knows her?)

## TURNS HEAD TO SOUNDS

About 4 months.

## PLAYS WITH HANDS

3-5 months.

## REACHES FOR AND GRASPS RATTLE

4-5 months.

## DROPS RATTLE ON PURPOSE

4-5 months or about a month after he grasps it.

## KNOWS HIS FRIENDS

5-8 months—The baby may go through a shy or "strange" time when he shrieks if strangers come near him.

## SWIMS

5-6 months—Watch, not only for when he begins to do this swimming trick, but also for when he stops doing it.

## ROLLS OVER ON PURPOSE

4-8 months—Usually, he turns from his stomach to his back first. Then, for weeks, he can't get back onto his stomach without help. (Sometimes very small babies squirm so much they flip over by accident.)

**SITS UP ALONE**
7–8 months.

**LOOKS IN MIRROR**
7–8 months.

**PICKS UP LITTLE THINGS**
7–9 months—He learns to pick up things likecorn flakes and raisins between his thumb and fingers. Since he puts everything into his mouth, it is important to keep him away from things that could choke him.

**WANTS TO FEED SELF**
7–8 months—He uses his fingers, of course.

**MOVES ON STOMACH (USUALLY BACKWARD)**
7–8 months.

**PULLS SELF UP TO STANDING POSITION**
7–11 months.

**CRAWLS**
8–11 months—This is when the baby starts getting into everything. Now is the time to put dangerous things up out of reach.

**PLAYS PAT-A-CAKE**
9–11 months.

**CRUISES**
10–12 months—A baby "cruises" when he walks around holding onto the furniture for support.

### WALKS ALONE

10–20 months—He stands alone before he begins to take steps. Even after he takes his first steps, he will often continue to crawl when he wants to go somewhere in a hurry.

### WAVES BYE-BYE

10–12 months.

### FIRST FEW WORDS

10–12 months—He says "no," "da-da," "mama," and a few other words. By now, however, he understands quite a bit of what you say to him.

### MANY SINGLE WORDS

15–20 months—At about this time, he knows many words, but he uses only one or two at a time.

### SIMPLE SENTENCES

18–24 months—Now he is really beginning to talk.

# Glossary

*amniotic fluid*
a clean, sweetened water in which the unborn baby lives

*amniotic sac*
the bag in the mother's womb which holds the fetus along with the water it lives in

*colic*
a kind of fussiness that causes some new babies to cry for no clear reason—usually at regular times each day

*to digest*
the stomach and intestines digest food by taking what the body needs and turning what is left into urine or bowel movements

*fetus (sounds like feetus)*
the unborn baby inside of its mother

*formula*
a drink for new babies, often made with cow's milk, sugar, and water

*gravity*
a force that pulls things toward earth and gives them weight

*to nurse*
to feed a baby at the breast

*oxygen*
the part of air which we need to live

*placenta*
a rootlike system that takes food and oxygen from the mother and feeds them to the unborn baby

*rhythm*
a regular beat

*umbilical cord*
a tube that connects the fetus to the placenta

*umbilicus*
belly button, the place where the umbilical cord was attached

*vocal cords*
the tissues that make noise when you speak

*water sac*
the amniotic sac

*to wean*
to make a baby drink from a bottle or cup instead of
from the breast

*womb (sounds like woom)*
the place in the mother which contains the amniotic sac
and the placenta

# Sources

Fraiberg, Selma H., *The Magic Years*. New York, Scribner, 1959.

Gruenberg, Sidonie Matsner, ed., *The New Encyclopedia of Child Care and Guidance*. Rev. ed. New York, Doubleday, 1966.

Guttmacher, Alan F., *Pregnancy and Birth*. Rev. ed. New York, Signet, 1962.

Liley, Margaret H., and Beth Day, *Modern Motherhood*. Rev. ed. New York, Random House, 1969.

Pryor, Karen, *Nursing Your Baby*. New York, Harper & Row, 1963.

Spock, Benjamin, *Baby and Child Care*. Rev. ed. New York, Pocket Books, 1968.

Spock, Benjamin, and Reinhart, John, *A Baby's First Year,* photographs by Wayne Miller. New York, Pocket Books, 1955.

Brackbill, Yvonne, ed., *Infancy and Early Childhood*. New York, The Free Press, 1967, *passim*.